D0975463

86157

225.95
Bull

Bull, Robert J.
Fishers of men

CONVERSE COUNTY LIBRARY
DOUGLAS, WYOMING

Roman World Of The First Century

FISHERS OF MEN

FISHERS OF MEN
The Way of the Apostles

Photographs by Gordon N. Converse

Text by Robert J. Bull and B. Cobbey Crisler

225.95
Bull

CONVERSE COUNTY LIBRARY.
DOUGLAS, WYOMING

86157

PRENTICE-HALL, INC., Englewood Cliffs, N.J.

Fishers of Men: The Way of the Apostles
by Gordon N. Converse, Robert J. Bull and B. Cobbey Crisler

Copyright © 1980 by Gordon N. Converse for photographs;
by Robert J. Bull and B. Cobbey Crisler for text

All rights reserved. No part of this book may be reproduced
in any form or by any means, except for the
inclusion of brief quotations in a review, without permission
in writing from the publisher. Address inquiries to Prentice-Hall, Inc.,
Englewood Cliffs, N.J. 07632

Printed in the United States

Prentice-Hall International, Inc., London
Prentice-Hall of Australia, Pty. Ltd., Sydney
Prentice-Hall of Canada, Ltd., Toronto
Prentice-Hall of India Private Ltd., New Delhi
Prentice-Hall of Japan, Inc., Tokyo
Prentice-Hall of Southeast Asia Pte. Ltd., Singapore
Whitehall Books Limited, Wellington, New Zealand

10 9 8 7 6 5 4 3 2 1

Converse, Gordon N.
Fishers of men.
1. Palestine—Description and travel—Views.
2. Mediterranean region—Description and travel—Views.
3. Apostles.
I. Bull, Robert J.   II. Crisler, B. Cobbey.   III. Title.
DS107.4.C666   225.9'5   80-23760
ISBN 0-13-319673-9

The authors wish to express appreciation for
permission to use the following photos:

p. 89 Courtesy of the Ephesus Museum, Selçuk, Turkey
p. 105 By Courtesy of the Israel Department of Antiquities and Museums
p. 123 Courtesy of the University of Michigan Library, Department of
Rare Books and Special Collections

To Marilyn and Bill Soukesian
who captured the vision of this volume from the start,
supported its research and accompanied
and encouraged us
every mile of the way.

ACKNOWLEDGMENTS

No volume makes its appearance without the support of an invisible team.
Our chief challenge is to convey sufficient appreciation to those on our special team
who provided the encouragement and means
to accomplish this book's *sine qua non*, research in six countries!
We owe much to Claire and Bill White;
to the Charles Stewart Harding Foundation of Flint, Michigan,
and The Foundation for Biblical Research and Preservation of Primitive Christianity
of Charlestown, New Hampshire.
To John Hughes, Charles Terrell, Robert Koehler, and Karin Logie
go our gratitude for smoothing intricacies of
preparation, travel, and financial planning.
Our search for ancient details in a modern land was spared enormous amounts of time and effort
through the courtesy and cooperation of Dr. Alev Coşkun, Minister of Tourism and Information for Turkey.
His personal interest, as well as that of his colleagues,
Yelman Emcan, Hüseyin Uluaslan, Ibrahim E. Büyükbenli, Reşat Tabak and Dr. Orhan Aytüg Taşyürek,
opened all doors in areas of their domain.
We owe thanks as well to the Joint Expedition to Caesarea Maritima
for the use of its vehicle in the exploration of both Greece and Turkey.
Finally, to Gene Permé, Hal Siegel, Edna Boschen,
editor Mariana Fitzpatrick, and other Prentice-Hall colleagues,
we extend much appreciation for shepherding this work along its way.
G.N.C.
R.J.B.
B.C.C.

INTRODUCTION

The fountainhead of Christianity that was Jesus' Palestine occupied an area about the size of New Hampshire. What a contrast for us to turn from this setting of our first book COME SEE THE PLACE: *The Holy Land Jesus Knew* and follow the route of Jesus' FISHERS OF MEN: *The Way of the Apostles*. Retracing the footsteps of those earliest Christians is an awesome pilgrimage, in terms of mileage alone.

Since the apostolic objective, as indicated by Paul, had been "to the Jew first, and also to the Greek" (Romans 1:16), we naturally were drawn in our journey towards vestiges of the diaspora. Some of these we searched for intentionally; others we stumbled upon. Many post-dated the apostles' connection with the sites; but all were signposts along the same ancient roads.

Paul, John, Peter, Philip and the other apostles had themselves followed the paths blazed by Judaism, finding their first audiences in the synagogues and under the shelter of an existing structure. Gradually, however, the impact of their teachings began to be felt by Gentiles. Indeed, had not Jesus called his first disciples "fishers of *men?*" (Mark 1:17)

Theirs was a way requiring courage, yet often tinged with trepidation. Thus Peter crossed the threshold of Cornelius' house in Caesarea Maritima, Philip faced the Ethiopian near Gaza, Paul and Barnabas, basing their authority on the Book of Isaiah, announced in Antioch of Pisidia, ". . . we turn to the Gentiles" (Acts 13:46) and John wrote to the seven churches in gentile Asia. Paul's ultimate insight on the universality of the Gospel message remains to challenge us today: "There is neither Jew nor Greek, there is neither bond nor free, there is neither male nor female; for ye are all one in Christ Jesus." (Galatians 3:28).

The pages that follow only hint at such radical stirrings in religious thought, presenting waymarks of the inexorable movement of Christianity westward. We have searched the Bible, archeological reports and visited sites of digs, past and current, but we have understood from the start that the "Way of the Apostles" was for these earliest Christians far more than geographical.

In this same spirit, it is our hope that this book records and conveys not only backgrounds but that deeper dimension which remains an inseparable part of those ancient and honored lands—the *lessons* lived and taught there by those "fishers of men."

Gordon N. Converse, Robert J. Bull and B. Cobbey Crisler

The former treatise have I made, O Theophilus, of all that Jesus began both to do and teach . . . And he said unto them, . . . ye shall be witnesses unto me both in Jerusalem, and in all Judaea, and in Samaria, and unto the uttermost part of the earth. And when he had spoken these things, while they beheld, he was taken up; and a cloud received him out of their sight. . . . Then returned they unto Jerusalem from the mount called Olivet, which is from Jerusalem a sabbath day's journey.   (Acts 1:1, 7–9, 12)

MOUNT CALLED OLIVET

From the traditional site on the summit of the Mount of Olives where Jesus commissioned his followers to go to the uttermost parts of the earth, all paths to the brook Kidron and across the valley to the gates of Jerusalem lead downhill. None are paved. Some wander by indirection amid the greenery and the centuries-old olive trees of the mountainside garden. Others, more direct, are wall-lined and stone-strewn, with the bedrock of the mountain exposed in places. All have been worn smooth by the passage of pilgrims and the wash of winter's rain.

Now Peter and John went up together into the temple at the hour of prayer, being the ninth hour. And a certain man lame from his mother's womb was carried, whom they laid daily at the gate of the temple which is called Beautiful . . . Who seeing Peter and John about to go into the temple asked an alms. . . . Then Peter said, Silver and gold have I none; but such as I have give I thee . . . And he took him by the right hand, and lifted him up: and immediately his feet and ancle bones received strength. . . . And as the lame man which was healed held Peter and John, all the people ran together unto them in the porch that is called Solomon's, greatly wondering. (Acts 3:1–3, 6, 7, 11)

SOLOMON'S PORCH

Rows of columns once adorned the top of the walls that surrounded the Jerusalem Temple built by Herod the Great. Of these, a double row stood on top of the eastern wall of the Temple complex and came to be called the Porch of Solomon. Archaeological evidence for this porch is lacking, but literary evidence—including the witness of Josephus—refers to the colonnade.

The Dome of the Rock (built on the traditional site of the Temple) and the top courses of the crenellated wall shown here are both of later construction; but some of the lower courses date from the time of Herod, and bore the wall once surmounted by the columns of Solomon's Porch.

CONVERSE COUNTY LIBRARY.
DOUGLAS, WYOMING

And Stephen, full of faith and power, did great wonders and miracles among the people.
. . . And they stoned Stephen . . . And Saul was consenting unto his death. And at that time
there was a great persecution against the church which was at Jerusalem; and they were
all scattered abroad throughout the regions of Judaea and Samaria, except the apostles.
(Acts 6:8; 7:59; 8:1)

WILDERNESS OF JUDAEA

Less than a half a day's journey east of Jerusalem lies the Wilderness of Judaea, a forbidding expanse
of limestone hills and steep ravines. Its inhospitable environment, including its lack of fresh water, supports
life only at a minimal level. There are no towns and few roads here. From the beginning of recorded
history the Wilderness has been the refuge of outlaws, those fleeing political and religious persecution,
or persons who have sought quiet, solitude, and isolation.

It was here that one religious community (considered to be the Essenes) gathered. Settling at
Qumran near the spring 'Ain Feshka along the western shore of the Dead Sea, they were able to live
removed from harassment and produce the body of manuscripts known as the Dead Sea Scrolls.
In Cave 4 (shown here), thousands of fragments from more than three hundred of these manuscripts,
including parts of every book of the Old Testament except the book of Esther, have been recovered.

Then Philip went down to the city of Samaria, and preached Christ unto them. . . . and many taken with palsies, and that were lame, were healed. And there was great joy in that city.
(Acts 8:5, 7–8)

CITY OF SAMARIA

Almost from the time of its founding as a capital city in the ninth century B.C. by Omri, King of Israel, Samaria suffered repeated capture and rebuilding. Under Herod the Great, however, when it was given the name *Sebaste* (Greek for *Augustus*), the city regained its status as an administrative center.

During the Roman period the major east-west street (the *decumanus maximus*), was lined with six hundred columns, some of which are shown here. Many of these seventeen-foot-high monolithic columns remain standing, two with their Corinthian capitals still intact. While the colonnades of the forty-foot-wide street may not have been erected until the second century A.D., the columns mark the location of the bazaar of the city from earliest times.

And Saul, yet breathing out threatenings and slaughter against the disciples of the Lord, went unto the high priest, and desired of him letters to Damascus to the synagogues, that if he found any of this way, whether they were men or women, he might bring them bound unto Jerusalem. And as he journeyed, he came near Damascus: and suddenly there shined round about him a light from heaven: And he fell to the earth, and heard a voice saying unto him, Saul, Saul, why persecutest thou me? (Acts 9:1–4)

ROAD TO DAMASCUS

The route north from Jerusalem to Damascus leads over the hill country of Judaea and Samaria, then northeast across the upper reaches of the Jordan Valley to the Golan Plateau and finally to the fertile plain on which Damascus lies. But by whatever road one traverses the varied terrain of this 150-mile trip, one cannot fail to be aware of the looming mass of Mount Hermon. Its 9,000-foot peak, usually snowcapped, is visible on occasion from the heights of Jerusalem, but its enormity compared to the surrounding hills is apparent only as one travels toward it on the Damascus road. Paul would have seen the snows of Hermon continually before him as he walked this route.

And Saul arose from the earth; and when his eyes were opened, he saw no man: but they led him by the hand, and brought him into Damascus. . . . And there was a certain disciple at Damascus, named Ananias . . . And the Lord said unto him, Arise, and go into the street which is called Straight, and inquire in the house of Judas for one called Saul, of Tarsus . . . that he might receive his sight. . . . And Ananias went his way, and entered into the house . . . And immediately there fell from his eyes as it had been scales: and he received sight forthwith, and arose, and was baptized.   (Acts 9:8, 10–12, 17, 18)

STREET CALLED STRAIGHT

Some vestiges of the classical city plan of Damascus still remain. The columns and gate shown here were part of the eighty-foot-wide street called Straight, which ran from east to west through the city, dividing it into almost equal northern and southern parts. Straight Street, however, does not run in a straight line across the city. It was laid out in three straight sections, with those to the east and west converging on the center one at slight angles. This double bend in the street, it is conjectured, was necessary in order to accommodate a large structure in existence when the city plan was laid out. In fact such a structure, the so-called palace, exists on the southern side of the center section of the street. The foundation of that structure predates the city plan and may mark where the Nabataean "governor under Aretas the king" (II Corinthians 11:32) had his residence in Paul's day.

Paul, an apostle, (not of men, neither by man, but by Jesus Christ, and God the Father, who raised him from the dead;) . . . I certify you, brethren, that the gospel which was preached of me is not after man. For I neither received it of man, neither was I taught it, but by the revelation of Jesus Christ. Neither went I up to Jerusalem to them which were apostles before me; but I went into Arabia, and returned again unto Damascus.   (Galatians 1:1, 11–12, 17)

In Damascus the governor under Aretas the king kept the city of the Damascenes with a garrison, desirous to apprehend me: And through a window in a basket was I let down by the wall, and escaped his hands.   (II Corinthians 11:32–33)

WALL OF DAMASCUS

Since Damascus was walled, access to the city was only through one of its gates, of which ancient Damascus had at least six. By closing them, the city could be sealed; by placing guards there, undesirables could be apprehended.

Defense considerations would not have permitted openings such as private exits or windows in the wall itself. The window from which Paul was lowered was probably in a building constructed on or near the top of the Damascus city wall.

The lower courses of stone shown here are part of the ancient city wall which surrounded Damascus.

20

Then after three years I went up to Jerusalem to see Peter, and abode with him fifteen days. But other of the apostles saw I none, save James the Lord's brother. (Galatians 1:18–19)

And he was with them coming in and going out at Jerusalem. And he spake boldly in the name of the Lord Jesus, and disputed against the Grecians: but they went about to slay him. Which when the brethren knew, they brought him down to Caesarea, and sent him forth to Tarsus. (Acts 9:28–30)

TARSUS

A commercial center and university seat, Tarsus produced several Stoic philosophers, poets, and grammarians and attracted travelers from throughout the known world. Cicero was Roman provincial governor in Tarsus. Cleopatra, dressed as Venus, came up the Cydnus River in a gilded barge with purple sails and silver oars to meet the inebriated Mark Antony waiting in the city. Plutarch noted it was to Tarsus that "Venus came to feast with Bacchus for the good of Asia."

Today, first-century Tarsus lies buried under as much as fourteen feet of alluvial deposit. The harbor and estuary which for centuries served as a haven for Mediterranean shipping are blocked and Tarsus is now separated from the sea by eleven miles of fertile fields.

West of the city there still exists a section of paved Roman road which traversed the Cilician Gates (the major pass through the Taurus mountains). This was the ancient route used by many conquerors of the world, like Sennacherib, Cyrus, and Alexander the Great. It linked Tarsus to the major cities of western Asia Minor, such as Smyrna and Ephesus, as well as to cities of the east, including Antioch, Damascus, and Jerusalem.

Born in this provincial capital, which fostered learning, this center of world trade, Paul could certainly say that he was "a citizen of no mean city." (Acts 21:39)

There was a certain man in Caesarea called Cornelius, a centurion of the band called the Italian band . . . He saw in a vision evidently about the ninth hour of the day an angel of God coming in to him; and saying unto him, Cornelius. . . . send men to Joppa, and call for one Simon, whose surname is Peter. . . . Then Peter went down to the men which were sent unto him from Cornelius; . . . And the morrow after they entered into Caesarea. And Cornelius waited for them, and had called together his kinsmen and near friends. . . . Then Peter opened his mouth, and said, Of a truth I perceive that God is no respecter of persons . . . While Peter yet spake these words, the Holy Ghost fell on all them which heard the word. . . . And he commanded them to be baptized in the name of the Lord. Then prayed they him to tarry certain days. (Acts 10:1, 3, 5, 21, 24, 34, 44, 48)

AQUEDUCT AT CAESAREA

A requisite of any ancient city was a pure and secure water supply. Herod the Great, when he planned and built Caesarea, constructed an aqueduct supported on six and a half miles of stone arches, to carry water from a spring on the southern slopes of Mount Carmel down to his capital city. Even as the aqueduct was built, however, it was recognized that this water source would not meet all of the needs of the city. As a result, the line of the aqueduct was extended to more remote springs located in the limestone foothills east of Caesarea. A tunnel three feet wide and four feet high by six and a half miles long was cut through solid rock of the foothills to an underground collection reservoir. When completed, the Caesarea aqueduct carried water at a constant rate and on a gradual downward slope for thirteen miles. Half the length of the channel ran through a rock-hewn tunnel, and the other half of its length was borne on a long line of graceful arches. This constant flow of spring water filled the public fountains and watered the public gardens of the city. Peter would have baptized Cornelius, "his kinsmen and near friends," with water supplied by the aqueduct shown here.

Then departed Barnabas to Tarsus, for to seek Saul: And when he had found him, he brought him unto Antioch. And it came to pass, that a whole year they assembled themselves with the church, and taught much people. And the disciples were called Christians first in Antioch. (Acts 11:25–26)

ANTIOCH

The remains of Antioch barely hint of the grandeur of a city which ranked third in the Roman Empire and had a population of half a million. Roman historian Ammianus Marcellinus called Antioch "the fair crown of the Orient," perhaps from the appearance of the crenellated walls that ringed it. The crumbling acropolis defense walls seen here, built by the Emperor Tiberius and later added to by the Emperor Justinian, still loom above what remains of the main part of the ancient city, located on the flood plain of the Orontes River below.

When this magnificent city was planned, its street system was so oriented that prevailing southwesterly winds from the Mediterranean ventilated the city. One broad avenue, built by Herod the Great, was over two miles long and ninety feet wide, and was adorned with a double row of Corinthian columns on each side of a central roadway. Sidewalks with tile-covered roofs protected pedestrians from summer sun and winter rain. At night the main street was torch lit.

Travelers approaching Antioch from the south in the latter part of the first century would have seen affixed to the southern gate of the city the great bronze Cherubim, taken from the Jewish Temple in Jerusalem by the Emperor Vespasian after the first Jewish Revolt. It hung facing Jerusalem as a mute reminder of Rome's answer to those who challenged her peace.

As they ministered to the Lord, and fasted, the Holy Ghost said, Separate me Barnabas and Saul for the work whereunto I have called them. . . . So they, being sent forth by the Holy Ghost, departed unto Seleucia . . . (Acts 13:2, 4)

SELEUCIA

Pilots of the Roman period looking for landfall, while still miles at sea, would have been able to sight the white marble Doric temple located on the Acropolis of Seleucia Pieria and know that in that direction lay a deep-water port, fresh water, and the western terminus of an overland trade route which extended from Antioch to the Far East. Seleucia, located on the Orontes River at the point where that navigable stream empties into the Mediterranean, was founded by Seleucus Nicator in the fourth century B.C., at about the same time he founded the city of Antioch farther up the river.

Seleucia served as the guardian of the eastern approaches to the Orontes Valley, and its harbor was the base of a Roman war fleet that protected shipping in the western end of the Mediterranean.

It was from the port of Seleucia that Paul and Barnabas set sail. According to a late fifth-century source, they had to wait in port three days for a ship. They would have sailed by the outer harbor breakwater under the looming mass of Mount Casios, seen here, before making for the open sea and Cyprus.

. . . and from thence they sailed to Cyprus. . . . and they had also John to their minister. . . .
Now when Paul and his company loosed from Paphos, they came to Perga in Pamphylia:
and John* departing from them returned to Jerusalem.   (Acts 13:4, 5, 13)

PERGA

First-century voyagers bound for Perga would have landed at the coastal port of Attalia, at which point
they would have sailed or been pulled up the Cestrus River to a wharf three miles east of the city of Perga.
    Entrance to the city was through three main gates. The southern gate (pictured here) was the
most massive, and the one that led to the major north-south street of the city (the *cardo maximus*).
This seventy-foot-wide avenue, adorned with a double colonnade, rose at a steady incline from a point
inside the gate up to the foot of the central high place of the city, the Acropolis. Paul, looking up toward
the citadel, would have seen a channeled course of water flowing down the center of the street,
its passage interrupted by a series of low dams which caused the formation of a descending series
of pools and waterfalls.

*John Mark (see Acts 15:37–38)

But when they departed from Perga, they came to Antioch in Pisidia, and went into the synagogue on the sabbath day, and sat down. And after the reading of the law and the prophets the rulers of the synagogue sent unto them, saying, Ye men and brethren, if ye have any word of exhortation for the people, say on. Then Paul stood up, and beckoning with his hand said, Men of Israel, and ye that fear God, give audience. . . . we declare unto you glad tidings, how that the promise which was made unto the fathers, God hath fulfilled the same unto us their children, in that he hath raised up Jesus again; as it is also written in the second psalm, Thou art my Son, this day have I begotten thee. . . . And the next sabbath day came almost the whole city together to hear the word of God.
(Acts 13:14–16, 32–33, 44; also quoting Psalms 2:7)

ANTIOCH IN PISIDIA

Although Pisidian Antioch lay on a major east-west Roman highway, first-century travelers heading north from the southern coast would have found no paved roads or bridges along the way. Paul, coming from Perga, would have encountered only trails—which ran first through marshy coastal lowlands, then up steep gorges formed by mountain streams—before reaching the 3,000-foot-high plateau, nearly one hundred miles inland, on which Antioch was built.

Founded by Seleucus Nicator (312–280 B.C.)—one of several cities he named for his father, Antiochus—Antioch had been incorporated primarily for military reasons into the Roman province of Galatia, and had by the time of the Emperor Augustus (27 B.C.–A.D. 14) been declared a free city and a Roman colony with the name Colonia Caesarea Antiochia. It had a strongly fortified city wall and a central forum dedicated to Augustus, in the midst of which stood a temple judged to have been one of the most aesthetically pleasing Greco-Roman structures known.

It was at the synagogue in Antioch in Pisidia that Paul first proclaimed publicly, "We turn to the Gentiles." No archaeological evidence of the synagogue has been found, but an epitaph dating from the third century A.D. states that Debora, a Jewish citizen of Antioch, had ancestors who held many honors in her fatherland.

The most evident remains of this ancient capital city, as seen today, are the dozen intact arches of the aqueduct which brought spring water to the city.

And it came to pass in Iconium, that they went both together into the synagogue of the Jews, and so spake, that a great multitude both of the Jews and also of the Greeks believed. . . . But the multitude of the city was divided . . . And when there was an assault made both of the Gentiles, and also of the Jews with their rulers, to use them despitefully, and to stone them, they were ware of it, and fled unto Lystra and Derbe, cities of Lycaonia, and unto the region that lieth round about: And there they preached the gospel. And there sat a certain man at Lystra, impotent in his feet, being a cripple from his mother's womb, who never had walked: The same heard Paul speak: who stedfastly beholding him, and perceiving that he had faith to be healed, said with a loud voice, Stand upright on thy feet. And he leaped and walked. (Acts 14:1, 4, 5–10)

LYSTRA

The site of Lystra was lost to history until 1885, when a Roman altar, inscribed with the city's name, was discovered in a field twenty-one miles southeast of ancient Iconium (Konya) near the modern Turkish village of Hatunsaray. The ancient road from Iconium ran just east of this site. Lystra's major city gate and its temple were probably located at that point.

This may be in part confirmed by the fact that the altar was found in the center of a level field east of the mound seen here, which contains the buried ruins of the city.

34

And when the people saw what Paul had done . . . they called Barnabas, Jupiter; and Paul, Mercurius, because he was the chief speaker. Then the priest of Jupiter, which was before their city, brought oxen and garlands unto the gates, and would have done sacrifice with the people. Which when the apostles, Barnabas and Paul, heard of, they rent their clothes, and ran in among the people, crying out, and saying, Sirs, why do ye these things? . . . And there came thither certain Jews from Antioch and Iconium, who persuaded the people, and, having stoned Paul, drew him out of the city, supposing he had been dead. Howbeit, as the disciples stood round about him, he rose up, and came into the city . . . (Acts 14:11, 12–15, 19, 20)

INSCRIPTION AT LYSTRA

The Roman altar, preserved in the Konya Archaeological Museum, contains a seven-line Latin inscription which reads:

> DIVUM AVG [USTUM]
> COL[ONIA] JUL[IA] FE
> LIX GEMINA
> LUSTRA
> CONSE
> CRAVIT
> D[ECRETO] D[EURIONUM]

This may be translated:

> Twice fortunate Lystra, a Julian colony dedicated to the divine Augustus.
> Decreed by the City Council.

The inscription indicates that Lystra had a temple dedicated to Augustus. It is possible, since Lystra was not a large town, that the Jupiter (Zeus) temple "which was before their city" and the temple to Augustus referred to in the altar inscription are the same.

DEVM·AVG?
COIVGEE
TERSEMINA
CONSE
CRAVIT
D·D·

. . . and the next day he departed with Barnabas to Derbe. And when they had preached the gospel to that city, and had taught many, they returned again to Lystra, and to Iconium, and Antioch, confirming the souls of the disciples, and exhorting them to continue in the faith, and that we must through much tribulation enter into the kingdom of God. (Acts 14:20–22)

DERBE

Until 1956 the location of the city of Derbe was not known. In that year a damaged block of soft limestone—weighing approximately one ton, and bearing a Greek inscription—was found on the side of an uninhabited mound in south central Turkey called Kerti Hüyük. The mound, approximately 65 feet high and 980 feet long by 650 feet wide, is strewn with pottery dating from the Iron Age through the Hellenistic and Roman periods. Some of the Roman potsherds found were of exceptionally fine quality. This suggests that Derbe had been occupied for several centuries, and that by the first century A.D. some of its inhabitants were affluent enough to possess imported Roman ceramic ware. The inscription, poorly preserved, contains sixteen lines of square-cut Greek text. The part of the inscription shown here begins with line seven (almost completely obliterated) and probably may be translated as follows:

> . . . the gods of Derbe having manifested themselves, the council and people,
> in the time of Cornelius Dexter, the governor [dedicated this altar].

Sextus Cornelius Dexter, the governor mentioned in the inscription, is known from other evidence to have been governor of Cilicia Isauria and Lycaonia in A.D. 157. The discovery that Derbe was located on the southeastern edge of the plain and border of Lycaonia means that Paul and Barnabas traveled farther south and east of Iconium than had hitherto been supposed.

And when they had ordained them elders in every church, and had prayed with fasting, they commended them to the Lord, on whom they believed. And after they had passed throughout Pisidia, they came to Pamphylia. And when they had preached the word in Perga, they went down into Attalia: And thence sailed to Antioch . . . And when they were come, and had gathered the church together, they rehearsed all that God had done with them, and how he had opened the door of faith unto the Gentiles. (Acts 14:23–25, 26, 27)

ATTALIA

The plain of Pamphylia on the southern coast of Turkey drops abruptly into the Mediterranean Sea, and the cliffs which mark that rugged shoreline extend uninterruptedly for about two hundred miles. Along that formidable coast there is to be found only one good—though small—natural harbor: Attalia. The city was founded circa 150 B.C. by Attalos II, King of Pergamum.

Part of the existing and extensive defense walls were probably standing when Paul visited Attalia. Vestiges of a round tower, which may have been an ancient lighthouse, stand at the end of the city wall on the south side of the harbor. It would have been from this harbor that Paul sailed to Antioch.

And some days after Paul said unto Barnabas, Let us go again and visit our brethren in every city where we have preached the word of the Lord, and see how they do. . . . And Paul chose Silas, and departed . . . And they passing by Mysia came down to Troas. (Acts 15:36, 40; 16:8)

Furthermore, when I came to Troas to preach Christ's gospel, and a door was opened unto me of the Lord, I had no rest in my spirit . . . (II Corinthians 2:12, 13)

And a vision appeared to Paul in the night; There stood a man of Macedonia, and prayed him, saying, Come over into Macedonia, and help us. (Acts 16:9)

HARBOR AT TROAS

The harbor of Troas, which included a shipyard for the building and repair of seagoing vessels, was enclosed by a massive rectangular system of defense walls one mile in depth and one and a half miles in breadth.

Columns and building materials robbed from the structures of the city lie strewn about the almost completely silted-up inner harbor.

ONTY LIBRARY.
OUGLAS, WYOMING

Therefore loosing from Troas, we came with a straight course to Samothracia, and the next day to Neapolis; and from thence to Philippi, which is the chief city of that part of Macedonia, and a colony: and we were in that city abiding certain days. (Acts 16:11–12)

NEAPOLIS TO PHILIPPI

The seaport of Neapolis was one of the stations on the Via Egnatia, the Roman military highway that ran from the Hellespont across Macedonia to Dyrrhachium, on the western shore of the Adriatic, and thence to Brundisium, on the opposite Italian shore. There the Via Egnatia continued north to join the Via Appia and the way to Rome. This was the most direct overland route between Asia and the capital of the Empire, as well as the most traveled Roman road between east and west. Disembarking at the port of Neapolis, Paul joined traffic on the Via Egnatia as the road, shown here, began its climb over Mount Symbolium to Philippi.

And on the sabbath we went out of the city by a river side, where prayer was wont to be made; and we sat down, and spake unto the women which resorted thither. And a certain woman named Lydia, a seller of purple, of the city of Thyatira, which worshipped God, heard us: whose heart the Lord opened, that she attended unto the things which were spoken of Paul. (Acts 16:13–14)

RIVERSIDE NEAR PHILIPPI

The Via Egnatia passed through the center of Philippi and exited the city on its western side through an arched gate. The remains of this western gate are still visible, and it is one of the few structures at Philippi that can be dated to the first century. A more elaborate marble arch symbolizing the political preeminence of Philippi as a Roman colony was erected in the first half of the first century a half mile west of the city, but no remains can be found. Paul and his company would have passed through both of these gates and traveled for less than a mile before arriving at the place where the Via Egnatia crosses a stream called the Gangites. Paving blocks of the highway can still be seen on both sides of the stream.

86157

. . . they caught Paul and Silas, and drew them into the marketplace unto the rulers, . . . and the magistrates rent off their clothes, and commanded to beat them. And when they had laid many stripes upon them, they cast them into prison, charging the jailor to keep them safely . . . And at midnight Paul and Silas prayed, and sang praises unto God . . . And suddenly there was a great earthquake, so that the foundations of the prison were shaken: and immediately all the doors were opened, and every one's bands were loosed.
(Acts 16:19, 22, 23, 25, 26)

MARKETPLACE AT PHILIPPI

Within the limits of the city of Philippi the Via Egnatia became the *decumanus maximus*, the major east-west street of the Roman city. On the south side of the main street, located in the center of Philippi, was the forum or marketplace, a rectangular court 328 feet long and 164 feet wide, paved in marble. The raised platform, seen here, was the podium from which public announcements were made, as well as the place where magistrates sat to hear cases brought before them. While the buildings at Philippi bear inscriptions that indicate they were erected during the reign of the Emperor Marcus Aurelius (A.D. 161–180), the general appearance of the second-century forum at Philippi was similar to, and the location of the podium probably the same as, those of the first century when Paul and Silas were brought there.

The circle divided into nine sections, scratched into the surface of one of the pavers of the forum in front of the podium at Philippi, is a game played with small pebbles used as counters. Similar games scratched into the surface of public structures are found all over the Roman Empire. One such game is found on the pavement of the Antonia Fortress in Jerusalem, where Jesus is considered by many to have been tried before Pilate.

Now when they had passed through Amphipolis and Apollonia . . .   (Acts 17:1)

LION OF AMPHIPOLIS

A colossal lion guards the western approaches to the remains of the city of Amphipolis, which lie within a full half-circle bend of the river Strymon, near where it empties into the Aegean Sea. Because of its protected location, Amphipolis was captured by Philip II of Macedon and made a fortress and a royal mint. Philip's son, Alexander the Great, made Amphipolis a naval base; and three of his most famous admirals— Nearchos, Androsthenes, and Laomedon—lived in the city. The lion monument, it is now thought, was probably a memorial to Laomedon.

When the Via Egnatia was laid through the city, the lion of Amphipolis would have been visible to the traffic passing by the point where the highway bridged the Strymon and continued west to Apollonia.

During the Balkan War, 1912–1913, trenching operations on the west bank of the Strymon River uncovered the shattered remains of the large lion and its pyramid base. Twenty-three years later, the lion of Amphipolis was reconstructed and reerected on a square base of ancient stones near the place by the river where it had originally been erected more than 2,250 years before.

. . . they came to Thessalonica, where was a synagogue of the Jews: And Paul, as his manner was, went in unto them, and three sabbath days reasoned with them out of the scriptures, opening and alleging, that Christ must needs have suffered, and risen again from the dead; and that this Jesus, whom I preach unto you, is Christ. And some of them believed . . . But the Jews which believed not . . . set all the city on an uproar . . . crying, These that have turned the world upside down are come hither also . . . (Acts 17:1–3, 4, 5, 6)

THESSALONICA

The column base and the remains of the patterned mosaic surface shown here are part of the east stoa in the Roman forum at Thessalonica. The stoa had Corinthian columns which extended along the top of a series of steps at the eastern end of a 295-foot-long by 230-foot-wide central paved court. Both steps and stoa extended in front of a large odeion, a theater where competition in music and poetry took place. While the odeion probably dates to the fourth century A.D., the east stoa was almost certainly in existence in the first century.

And they that conducted Paul brought him unto Athens: and receiving a commandment unto Silas and Timotheus for to come to him with all speed, they departed. Now while Paul waited for them at Athens, his spirit was stirred in him, when he saw the city wholly given to idolatry. (Acts 17:15–16)

ACROPOLIS OF ATHENS

It is probable that Paul journeyed from Berea, twenty-five miles southeast to the coast of the Gulf of Thermaikos, and there embarked for Athens. If so, he would have sailed south along the east coast of the Aegean Sea to the southern end of the Attic peninsula. High on the headland to starboard as the vessel rounded Cape Sounion he would have seen the stark white Doric Temple of Poseidon. Heading north toward Piraeus, the port of Athens, the eyes of all aboard ship would have been intent on watching for the sun's reflection as it glanced off the spear point or the burnished bronze helmet of the thirty-foot-high statue of Athena Promachos which stood on the heights of the Acropolis as much as thirty miles away.

From whatever direction he approached Athens, Paul would have seen from afar the temple-adorned heights of the Acropolis—then, only a remnant of the former "violet-crowned" city of Pericles. Sacked in 86 B.C. by Sulla's Roman army, Athens had never been rebuilt to its former glory. Even so, Paul would have beheld the temple of the Wingless Victory, the Propylaea, the intact Parthenon, the Erechtheion, and the theatre of Dionysus, among many others. On every hand were temples, niches, groves, theatres, shrines—all adorned and filled with representations of gods and goddesses. Acts 17:16 indicates that Paul was exasperated at the idolatry he saw about him. Pliny estimated that in the first century A.D. there were still as many as twenty thousand statues within the city.

Therefore disputed he in the synagogue with the Jews, and with the devout persons, and in the market daily with them that met with him. Then certain philosophers of the Epicureans, and of the Stoicks, encountered him. And some said, What will this babbler say? . . . He seemeth to be a setter forth of strange gods . . . (Acts 17:17, 18)

MARKET OF ATHENS

Northwest of the Acropolis, near the gate by which the road from Piraeus entered Athens, lay the *agora* or market, the open area which was the civic and commercial center of the city. Here—as in every Greek city—citizens, merchants, government officials, travelers, philosophers, and jugglers gathered to hear the news of the day, transact business, engage in philosophical and political debate, or be entertained. In Athens, the *agora* was flanked by stoas, long colonnaded structures which housed shops and public offices, the shaded porticos of which served as convenient places for conversation, debate, business, or idle talk. To the Greek mind, a city without an *agora* was barbarian. Indeed, the *agora* was held to be of such value that its limits were carefully defined, and any person convicted of a serious offense or whose entry would be against the best interests of the community was denied access.
At the south end of the Athenian *agora* a small marble slab inscribed in Greek has been uncovered. In translation the inscription reads, "I am the boundary of the Agora."

Beneath the heights of the Acropolis, the structure that loomed immediately over the *agora* in the first century when Paul spoke there, even as it does today, was the Temple of Hephaestus, the god of craftsmen. The best preserved of the large ancient Greek temples, it may have been constructed by the same architect who built the Doric Temple of Poseidon which Paul would have seen as he sailed by the headland at Cape Sounion.

*And they took him, and brought him unto Areopagus, saying, May we know what this new
doctrine, whereof thou speakest, is? . . . (For all the Athenians and strangers which were
there spent their time in nothing else, but either to tell, or to hear some new thing.) Then Paul
stood in the midst of Mars' hill, and said, Ye men of Athens, I perceive that in all things
ye are too superstitious.* (Acts 17:19, 21–22)

AREOPAGUS

West of the Propylaea, the main entrance to the Acropolis, stands a 377-foot-high hill called the Areopagus,
Mars' hill, named after Ares, the god of war. Even prior to the Golden Age of Greece, this hill was the
place of assembly for the aristocratic governing body of Athens. Later, however, the location lost some of
its importance and became the occasional meeting place of a court that tried homicides. Rock-hewn
benches on three sides of a rough courtyard that marks the assembly place can still be seen.

From the top of the Areopagus in the foreground, Paul and those who heard him would have
been constantly aware of the Acropolis that towered above and beside them to the east. At its center was
the Parthenon, one of the most beautiful and revered temples made by the hand of man.

Every four years a lengthy Panathenaic procession made its way from the city gate through the
agora, up the western side of the Acropolis, through the Propylaea, and to the Erechtheion, where a
new white robe was offered to the idol of Athena. Paul may not have observed the actual procession, but
its entire course was exquisitely depicted in marble bas-relief around the frieze of the Parthenon
(the so-called Elgin Marbles, now in the British Museum)—a reminder to all who observed it that
the goddess Athena of the Acropolis was the center of Athens, of Greece, and of civilization itself.

*For as I passed by, and beheld your devotions, I found an altar with this inscription,
TO THE UNKNOWN GOD. Whom therefore ye ignorantly worship, him declare I unto you.
God that made the world and all things therein, seeing that he is Lord of heaven and
earth, dwelleth not in temples made with hands . . . For in him we live, and move,
and have our being; as certain also of your own poets have said, For we are also
his offspring.*   (Acts 17:23–24, 28)

TEMPLES MADE WITH HANDS

The Temple of Hephaestus, with all thirty-four of the fluted Doric columns in its peristyle intact and its roof preserved, was built in the fifth century B.C. From the depths of the east porch of the Temple of Hephaestus, one can look out between the Doric columns across the open area to the stoa and the Athenian *agora*. The heights of the Acropolis and the Parthenon can be seen beyond. Although no altar "to the Unknown God" has been unearthed in Athens, similar altars have been discovered in other cities, such as Pergamum.

In his Mars' hill address, Paul apparently quotes a line from the Greek sage Epimenides, "For by him we live, move, and exist" as well as a line from Aratus' *Phaenomena*, "For we are also his offspring."

After these things Paul departed from Athens, and came to Corinth; and found a certain Jew named Aquila, born in Pontus, lately come from Italy, with his wife Priscilla; (because that Claudius had commanded all Jews to depart from Rome:) and came unto them.
And because he was of the same craft, he abode with them, and wrought: for by their occupation they were tentmakers. (Acts 18:1–3)

CORINTH

In the first century the road from Lechaion, Corinth's port on the Ionian Sea, was column-lined as it entered Corinth. Within the city it terminated at a grand staircase which led up to an ornate gateway formed by a massive marble arch surmounted by two great bronze chariots. Through that splendid gateway travelers would have entered into a vast two-level *agora* 656 feet long east and west by 328 feet wide north and south, all paved in marble.

Suetonius in his *Life of Claudius* (XXX.4) may refer to the same banishment of Jews from Rome when he writes, "Since the Jews constantly made disturbances at the instigation of Chrestus, he (Claudius) expelled them from Rome."

*And he reasoned in the synagogue every sabbath, and persuaded the Jews and the Greeks.
. . . and entered into a certain man's house, named Justus, one that worshipped God,
whose house joined hard to the synagogue. And Crispus, the chief ruler of the synagogue,
believed on the Lord with all his house; and many of the Corinthians hearing believed, and
were baptized.*   (Acts 18:4, 7–8)

SYNAGOGUE AT CORINTH

In 1898 the broken inscribed limestone lintel shown here was found in Corinth at the point where the steps
on the central Lechaion road lead up to the *agora* of the city. The partial inscription may be translated:

Synagogue of the Hebrews

The style of the letters in the inscription suggest that the lintel was part of the door of a synagogue
in use in the second century A.D. While there is no way of knowing whether or not this was the
synagogue in which Paul spoke, the lintel is clear evidence of a Jewish community in Corinth. Further,
since the stone on which the inscription was found is large and heavy, there is reason to believe that it
remained near the place where it fell when the building of which it was a part was destroyed. That would
suggest that the synagogue of Corinth was on the central major street of the city near the marketplace.

And when Gallio was the deputy of Achaia, the Jews made insurrection with one accord against Paul, and brought him to the judgment seat, saying, This fellow persuadeth men to worship God contrary to the law. And when Paul was now about to open his mouth, Gallio said unto the Jews . . . if it be a question of words and names, and of your law, look ye to it; for I will be no judge of such matters. And he drave them from the judgment seat. Then all the Greeks took Sosthenes, the chief ruler of the synagogue, and beat him before the judgment seat. And Gallio cared for none of those things. (Acts 18:12–13, 14, 15–17)

JUDGMENT SEAT IN CORINTH

In the middle of the central division of the Corinthian *agora* stood an elevated platform or *bema*. This imposing structure faced the lower and southern half of the *agora* with its 328-foot-long stoa, as well as the gateway of the road that led to Cenchrea, Corinth's port on the Aegean Sea.

In front of the *bema*, shown here with the peaks of the Acrocorinth rising behind it to the south, Paul probably faced his Jewish accusers before Roman Proconsul Lucius Junius Gallio, friend of the Emperor Claudius and brother of the Stoic philosopher and author Seneca.

O ye Corinthians . . . Be ye not unequally yoked together with unbelievers: for what fellowship hath righteousness with unrighteousness? . . . or what part hath he that believeth with an infidel? And what agreement hath the temple of God with idols? for ye are the temple of the living God . . . Wherefore come out from among them, and be ye separate, saith the Lord . . . (II Corinthians 6:11, 14, 15, 16, 17)

TEMPLE OF APOLLO

Only seven Doric columns remain of the thirty-eight that formed the peristyle of the Temple of Apollo at Corinth. Built in the sixth century B.C., it remains one of the two oldest temples in Greece with standing columns. Constructed on the highest point within the city of Corinth proper, its classic form was visible to travelers on the north-south road from both sides of the Corinthian Isthmus.

In 146 B.C. the city was sacked and largely destroyed by the Romans. For a full century the remains of Corinth lay deserted, until Julius Caesar in 44 B.C. encouraged new colonists to settle there. They rebuilt the city, reusing much of its stone. The Temple of Apollo was one of the few structures in the city that escaped both this complete destruction and the later stone-robbing efforts. When Paul came to Corinth in the first century, he would have seen a newly-built city with only two or three of the buildings from the Greek classical period still standing. The Apollo Temple was one.

*As concerning therefore the eating of those things that are offered in sacrifice unto idols,
we know that an idol is nothing in the world, and that there is none other God but one. . . .
But meat commendeth us not to God: for neither, if we eat, are we the better; neither, if we eat
not, are we the worse. . . . What say I then? . . . Whatsoever is sold in the shambles,
that eat, asking no question for conscience sake . . . But if any man say unto you, This is
offered in sacrifice unto idols, eat not for his sake that shewed it, and for conscience sake . . .
Whether therefore ye eat, or drink, or whatsoever ye do, do all to the glory of God.*
(I Corinthians 8:4, 8; 10:19, 25, 28, 31)

SHAMBLES AT CORINTH

Within the long south stoa on the lower level of the Corinthian *agora*, more than thirty shops have been
excavated. In each, a shaft led to an underground water course, which was so arranged that perishable
goods could be kept cool by flowing water. The nature of all the shops is not known, but scratched on
a stone used as a doorjamb in one is a crude Greek inscription which translated reads, "Lucius the
butcher." A second inscription, likewise found in the stoa, but more formally and precisely incised,
contains the Latin word MACELLU[M], which may be translated to mean *shambles* or *meat market*.
Paul uses the parallel Greek term when he speaks of "whatsoever is sold in the shambles."

Know ye not that they which run in a race run all, but one receiveth the prize? So run, that ye may obtain. . . . Now they do it to obtain a corruptible crown; but we an incorruptible. I therefore so run, not as uncertainly . . . But I keep under my body, and bring it into subjection: lest that by any means, when I have preached to others, I myself should be a castaway. (I Corinthians 9:24, 25, 26, 27)

. . . forgetting those things which are behind, and reaching forth unto those things which are before, I press toward the mark for the prize of the high calling of God in Christ Jesus. (Philippians 3:13–14)

ISTHMIAN GAMES

In early Greek literature, Isthmia refers to a sports festival held every two years near the sanctuary of Poseidon on the Isthmus of Corinth. Near the temple, the remains of a 630-foot-long stadium has been uncovered; within the stadium two distinct types of starting gates for runners have been found.
In the simpler type of gate the starting line consisted of deep grooves cut into stone sills set across the track. By means of the grooves the runner's foot was afforded a secure place to begin the race.
The other type of gate is earlier and more complex. From a central well-shaped hole, approximately 3 feet in diameter, 16 inscribed lines radiate outward to bronze fittings designed to support wooden gates.
It is conjectured that by means of cords, the starter of the race—standing in the well-shaped hole seen here—could control the fall of the starting gates and thereby the start of the runners.

Then spake the Lord to Paul in the night by a vision, Be not afraid, but speak, and hold not thy peace: For I am with thee, and no man shall set on thee to hurt thee: for I have much people in this city.   (Acts 18:9–10)

Erastus abode at Corinth . . .   (II Timothy 4:20)

Gaius mine host, and of the whole church, saluteth you. Erastus the chamberlain of the city saluteth you, and Quartus a brother.   (Romans 16:23)

ERASTUS INSCRIPTION

In a small open area at the northern end of a street that runs beside the theatre at Corinth lies a large limestone block deeply incised with the following inscription:

ERASTUS·PRO·AED
S·P·STRAVIT

This can be reconstructed to read:

ERASTUS PRO AEDILITATE SUA PECUNIA STRAVIT

which may be translated to mean:

Erastus, in return for his aedilship, at his own expense,
laid the pavement

This inscription indicates that Erastus was the Corinthian commissioner of public works when the street was laid. It is possible that he was the same person Paul speaks of as being "the chamberlain of the city" and a member of the Corinthian Christian community.

And Paul after this tarried there yet a good while, and then took his leave of the brethren, and sailed thence into Syria, and with him Priscilla and Aquila; having shorn his head in Cenchrea: for he had a vow. (Acts 18:18)

HARBOR AT CENCHREA

Cenchrea, the port of Corinth, lay on the Aegean side of the Isthmus of Corinth; it was the harbor through which all Corinthian traffic to and from the east passed. The moles that defined the harbor of Cenchrea are now submerged, as are many of the structures immediately adjoining the port, since tectonic action has caused the land in the area of the harbor to subside in some places as much as six feet. On a pier that joins the southwestern mole of the harbor lies a partially sunken sanctuary of Isis, the Egyptian goddess of motherhood and fertility. It was in the submerged apse of Isis' sanctuary that there were recently found 100 three- by six-foot glass panels depicting buildings along the sea, human figures, flowers, and birds, all still in their shipping cases where they were left in the fourth century A.D.

And when he had landed at Caesarea, and gone up, and saluted the church, he went down to Antioch. (Acts 18:22)

CAESAREA

Approximately twenty years ago, the point of a farmer's plow struck a sculpted purple stone some 250 feet east of the moat of the Crusader fortress at Caesarea, the site of the Roman and Byzantine provincial capital of Palestine. When fully uncovered, the stone proved to be part of an 8½-foot-high seated figure weighing nine tons and carved from a block of purple Egyptian rhyolite. There are indications that separately formed legs, hands, and a head were once attached to the figure and a white marble hand thought to have been part of the completed statue has been found.

Since the sculpture represented an emperor's purple toga and the style of the carving was that of the second century, it has been concluded that the statue was of a second century emperor, probably the Emperor Hadrian (A.D. 117-138). Subsequent excavation beside the statue uncovered an esplanade which determined the eastern limit of the city's forum. Josephus had recorded statuary of this quality at Caesarea in his day. By the second century, the capital of Palestine which Herod the Great had laid out *de novo* in the last half of the first century B.C. must have been amply and magnificently decorated.

And after he had spent some time there, he departed, and went over all the country of Galatia and Phrygia in order, strengthening all the disciples. (Acts 18:23)

For I would that ye knew what great conflict I have for you, and for them at Laodicea, and for as many as have not seen my face in the flesh. . . . And when this epistle is read among you, cause that it be read also in the church of the Laodiceans; and that ye likewise read the epistle from Laodicea. (Colossians 2:1; 4:16)

LAODICEA

Originally called Diospolis, the city was named Laodicea when it was refounded in the third century B.C. by Antiochus II as a military stronghold. It was not until the Roman period, however, that the city grew in fame and financial strength from trade in the world-renowned glossy black wool which the region produced. This prized wool was woven directly into seamless clokes which had a central opening and were pulled on over the head (the cloke of II Timothy 4:13). Based on the wool trade, Laodicea became a banking and mercantile center.

Paul's letter to the Colossians implies he had not visited Laodicea but was sensitive to the needs of its church. Laodicea was at the height of its success and wealth during Paul's Phrygian ministry. Visitors would have seen—among the many large, ornate public buildings—the theatre shown here. The white slopes visible above the theatre are on the opposite bank of the Lycus River Valley and mark the location of Hierapolis, where an enormous ten-thousand-gallon-per-minute thermal spring sends hot (95°F) mineral-bearing water cascading down the valley side, producing a series of glistening white pools and terraces visible for miles. Colossae, to which Paul wrote, was on the same side of the valley as Laodicea, and some twelve miles distant to the southeast.

Laodicea suffered from a major earthquake during the reign of Emperor Tiberius (A.D. 14–37) and another even greater one in A.D. 60. A third disastrous earthquake occurred in A.D. 494 and ended the prosperity of the city.

Beware lest any man spoil you through philosophy and vain deceit, after the tradition of men, after the rudiments of the world, and not after Christ. . . . Epaphras, who is one of you, a servant of Christ, saluteth you . . . For I bear him record, that he hath a great zeal for you, and them that are in Laodicea, and them in Hierapolis. (Colossians 2:8; 4:12, 13)

HIERAPOLIS

Christianity reached Hierapolis just prior to the great earthquake of A.D. 60, which destroyed the city. It is from the period of extensive rebuilding that we have our earliest evidence of the growth of the Christian community. Philip the evangelist and his four daughters, who were prophetesses (Acts 21:9), are said to have lived in Hierapolis. Papias, the Christian author who delighted in collecting oral traditions about Jesus and the apostles, lived and wrote there. One reference in the Talmud probably refers to the absorption of the Jewish community at Hierapolis into the strong Gentile influence there in the words "The wines and the battles of Phrygia have separated the ten tribes from Israel."

The cemetery gives ample evidence of the wealth of the citizenry of Hierapolis; and because many of the more than one thousand tombs are inscribed, there are clues to the social, ethnic, and religious makeup of the population. The seven-branched menorah, carved in the end of a sarcophagus lid, evidences the presence of Jewish residents at Hierapolis. To the left of the menorah is a poorly carved Greek inscription, which may be translated:

Belonging to the Jews

*And a certain Jew named Apollos, born at Alexandria, an eloquent man, and mighty in the
scriptures, came to Ephesus. . . . And he began to speak boldly in the synagogue . . .
For he mightily convinced the Jews, and that publickly, shewing by the scriptures that Jesus
was Christ. . . . And it came to pass, that, while Apollos was at Corinth, Paul having passed
through the upper coasts came to Ephesus . . . disputing daily in the school of one Tyrannus.
And this continued by the space of two years; so that all they which dwelt in Asia heard
the word of the Lord Jesus, both Jews and Greeks. And God wrought special miracles
by the hands of Paul . . .*   (Acts 18:24, 26, 28; 19:1, 9, 10–11)

EPHESUS

From "the country of Galatia and Phrygia" (Acts 18:23), Paul would probably have traveled along the
road beside the Maeander River as far as Magnesia, and thence to Ephesus. Entering the city by the
Magnesian Gate, the same gate used in the elaborate annual birthday procession of the goddess Artemis
("Diana of the Ephesians"), Paul would have traveled down the street seen here. Ignatius of Antioch, on his
way to martyrdom at Rome, called this marble-paved roadway, lined with columns and marble buildings,
"the passageway of those who are slain unto God," referring to the Christians who had walked this street
on their way to martyrdom.

And the same time there arose no small stir about that way. For a certain man named Demetrius, a silversmith, which made silver shrines for Diana, brought no small gain unto the craftsmen; whom he called together with the workmen of like occupation, and said, Sirs, ye know that by this craft we have our wealth. Moreover ye see and hear, that not alone at Ephesus, but almost throughout all Asia, this Paul hath persuaded and turned away much people, saying that they be no gods, which are made with hands: So that not only this our craft is in danger to be set at nought; but also that the temple of the great goddess Diana should be despised, and her magnificence should be destroyed, whom all Asia and the world worshippeth. (Acts 19:23–27)

TEMPLE OF DIANA

One of the seven wonders of the ancient world, the Temple of Artemis or Diana, stood at Ephesus on the estuary of the Cayster River, open to the Icarium Sea. Today the broken remains of this renowned structure lie distributed across a swampy field. Structures dating back to the eighth century B.C. have stood on the site, but the temple that gave the Artemision its fame was begun about 550 B.C. and took 120 years to build. A madman named Herostratus, seeking to immortalize his name, burned the temple on the night Alexander the Great was born. The Temple of Diana, which was standing when Paul lived in Ephesus, was designed by Dinocrates of Alexandria, and was begun about 350 B.C. The podium on which it stood was over 400 feet long and nearly 240 feet wide. The temple, with Ionic columns over 55 feet high, was 360 feet long and 180 feet wide. It stood until A.D. 262, when it was burned by the invading Goths. Even then, in spite of the growing influence of Christianity, it was rebuilt. During the more than 1,300-year history of temples to Artemis at Ephesus, all were apparently destroyed by the hand of man, none by the earthquake action that leveled so many of the classical structures in Asia Minor. This is a tribute to the original designers, who apparently considered marshy ground better foundation in earthquake regions than bedrock.

And when they heard these sayings, they were full of wrath, and cried out, saying, Great is Diana of the Ephesians.   (Acts 19:28)

DIANA OF THE EPHESIANS

Artemis (Diana) of Ephesus was a nature deity, a goddess of fertility with many of the characteristics of the ancient Asian diety, the Great Mother, and not unlike the Phrygian Cybele or the Phoenician Astarte. Statues that represent her are found distributed from one end of the Mediterranean to the other.

A coin displayed in the Ephesus Museum at Selçuk, Turkey, has on its reverse DIANA EPHESIA, Diana of the Ephesians, and a representation of the goddess. Alleged not to have been made with hands, but rather to have descended from heaven as a meteor, she was believed by thousands to perform miracles, cure the ill, regulate commerce, solve domestic difficulties, and afford refuge within her temple to all who were pursued or in danger.

Beware lest any man spoil you through philosophy and vain deceit, after the tradition of men, after the rudiments of the world, and not after Christ. . . . Epaphras, who is one of you, a servant of Christ, saluteth you . . . For I bear him record, that he hath a great zeal for you, and them that are in Laodicea, and them in Hierapolis. (Colossians 2:8; 4:12, 13)

HIERAPOLIS

Christianity reached Hierapolis just prior to the great earthquake of A.D. 60, which destroyed the city. It is from the period of extensive rebuilding that we have our earliest evidence of the growth of the Christian community. Philip the evangelist and his four daughters, who were prophetesses (Acts 21:9), are said to have lived in Hierapolis. Papias, the Christian author who delighted in collecting oral traditions about Jesus and the apostles, lived and wrote there. One reference in the Talmud probably refers to the absorption of the Jewish community at Hierapolis into the strong Gentile influence there in the words "The wines and the battles of Phrygia have separated the ten tribes from Israel."

The cemetery gives ample evidence of the wealth of the citizenry of Hierapolis; and because many of the more than one thousand tombs are inscribed, there are clues to the social, ethnic, and religious makeup of the population. The seven-branched menorah, carved in the end of a sarcophagus lid, evidences the presence of Jewish residents at Hierapolis. To the left of the menorah is a poorly carved Greek inscription, which may be translated:

Belonging to the Jews

And the whole city was filled with confusion: and having caught Gaius and Aristarchus, men of Macedonia, Paul's companions in travel, they rushed with one accord into the theatre. (Acts 19:29)

THEATRE AT EPHESUS

At the eastern end of the colonnaded street that led from the harbor of Ephesus, and built into the western slope of Mount Pion, loomed the massive theatre of Ephesus. Begun during the reign of the Emperor Claudius (A.D. 51–54) and completed during the reign of the Emperor Trajan (A.D. 98-117), the theatre was still in the process of construction during Paul's visit to Ephesus. Twenty-five thousand people could be seated there in three levels of twenty-two rows each, all on white marble seats. The colonnaded marble street leading to the theatre is thirty-five feet across. On the outside of each of the rows of columns a sixteen-foot-wide mosaic pavement ran the length of the street. The large column with composite capital standing on a pedestal, seen here, is the one remaining column of four erected by the sixth century A.D. The pedestal base of another can be seen to the left. On top of each of the columns there once stood a statue of one of the four evangelists.

And when Paul would have entered in unto the people, the disciples suffered him not.
And certain of the chief of Asia, which were his friends, sent unto him, desiring him that
he would not adventure himself into the theatre.   (Acts 19:30–31)

ASIARCHS

Paul was advised by "certain of the chief of Asia," or Asiarchs, not to venture into the crowd of rioters
in the theatre at Ephesus. An Asiarch was a provincial official charged with the guardianship of the rites of
the Imperial Roman cult and of the festivals at which the emperor was adored. The name of one of
these officials found on the inscription shown here, which was uncovered at Ephesus, may be translated:

   P[ublius] Ailios Martiales, Asiarch

CONVERSE COUNTY LIBRARY
DOUGLAS, WYOMING

And when the townclerk had appeased the people, he said, Ye men of Ephesus, what man is there that knoweth not how that the city of the Ephesians is a worshipper of the great goddess Diana, and of the image which fell down from Jupiter? . . . ye ought to be quiet, and to do nothing rashly. . . . if Demetrius, and the craftsmen which are with him, have a matter against any man, the law is open, and there are deputies . . . For we are in danger to be called in question for this day's uproar . . . And when he had thus spoken, he dismissed the assembly. (Acts 19:35, 36, 38, 40, 41)

INSIDE THE THEATRE

The uppermost of the 66 rows of seats in the theatre of Ephesus rises 100 feet above the orchestra level. From this vantage point, a first-century observer could enjoy a commanding view of the harbor of Ephesus, the 1,700-foot-long marble-paved and column-lined street that ran from the harbor to the city, and the 132-foot-wide multistoried stage that extended across the front of the theatre. Lit by the setting sun, the theatre enabled 24,000 spectators to witness plays, mimes, and pantomimes, or to take part in public assemblies. It was in this theatre that irate merchants and their friends started a demonstration against Paul and his companions which was quelled only by the intervention of local government authorities.

And after the uproar was ceased, Paul called unto him the disciples, and embraced them, and departed for to go into Macedonia. . . . as he was about to sail into Syria, . . . These going before tarried for us at Troas. . . . where we abode seven days. And upon the first day of the week . . . Paul preached unto them, ready to depart on the morrow; and continued his speech until midnight. And there were many lights in the upper chamber, where they were gathered together. And there sat in a window a certain young man named Eutychus, being fallen into a deep sleep: and as Paul was long preaching, he sunk down with sleep, and fell down from the third loft, and was taken up dead. And Paul went down, and . . . said, . . . his life is in him. . . . And they brought the young man alive . . . (Acts 20:1, 3, 5, 6, 7–9, 10, 12)

TROAS

Troas was built in 310 B.C. by Antigonus on the shore of the Aegean Sea. It lay some fourteen miles southwest of the ruins of Troy (Ilium), the fabled city of Homer's *Iliad*. Located on the western shore of Asia, Troas was the nearest port to mainland Greece and Europe. Called Alexandria Troas in honor of Alexander the Great, it had become a Roman possession by 133 B.C. Suetonius states that Julius Caesar so admired Troas, in part because of its nearness to Troy, that he planned to make it the capital of the Roman Empire. The city included elaborate buildings, such as a bath and theatre, the remains of which can still be seen. Other structures—including the aqueduct, stadium, *agora*, and a Doric temple—are known only through literary references.

And we went before to ship, and sailed unto Assos, there intending to take in Paul:
for so had he appointed, minding himself to go afoot. And when he met with us at Assos,
we took him in, and came to Mitylene. (Acts 20:13, 14)

ROAD TO ASSOS

Paul walked from Troas to Assos, a journey of thirty miles which would have taken about eight hours.
On that journey he would have approached Assos from the north by way of the Roman highway shown
here. Hours before he got there, however, he would have been able to view, sharply outlined on the horizon
above the sea, the steep hill of volcanic rock on which the fortified city of Assos was built. On the
seaside directly beneath the heights of Assos lay the now filled-in harbor from which Paul sailed to
Mitylene, chief city of the Aegean island of Lesbos.

And we sailed thence, and came the next day over against Chios; and the next day we arrived at Samos, and tarried at Trogyllium; and the next day we came to Miletus. For Paul had determined to sail by Ephesus, because he would not spend the time in Asia . . . And from Miletus he sent to Ephesus, and called the elders of the church. And when they were come to him, he said unto them, . . . behold, I go bound in the spirit unto Jerusalem, not knowing the things that shall befall me there . . .   (Acts 20:15, 16, 17, 22)

MILETUS

The theatre at Miletus, with its 460 feet of frontal length, and a seating capacity of over 15,000, was built into the side of a 100-foot-high hill which was originally the acropolis of the city. Situated on a peninsula between two bodies of water—the Bay of Lions and the Bay of the Theatre—its prominent location and size were indicative of its importance to the life of the city. A first-century visitor to Miletus could not help but be impressed with the architectural mastery shown in the construction of this structure, acknowledged to be one of the finest theatres in Asia Minor.

*Of the Jews five times received I forty stripes save one. Thrice was I beaten with rods,
once was I stoned, thrice I suffered shipwreck, a night and a day I have been in the deep;
in journeyings often . . . in perils of robbers, in perils by mine own countrymen, in perils by
the heathen . . . in perils among false brethren; in weariness and painfulness . . .
in hunger and thirst . . . in cold and nakedness. Beside . . . the care of all the churches.*
(II Corinthians 11:24, 25, 26, 27, 28)

*But none of these things move me, neither count I my life dear unto myself, so that I might
finish my course with joy . . . remember the words of the Lord Jesus, how he said, It is more
blessed to give than to receive. And when he had thus spoken, he kneeled down, and
prayed with them all. . . . And they accompanied him unto the ship.* (Acts 20:24, 35, 36, 38)

INSCRIPTION AT MILETUS

Certain sections of seats in the theatre at Miletus were permanently reserved. The name of the groups
or organizations that owned or had paid for the seating was found inscribed in the stone of the seats.
Part of one row of seats, for example, was reserved for ironworkers, another for goldsmiths. Carved into
the fifth row of seats on the right as one enters the theatre are words which may be translated:

THE PLACE OF THE JEWS AND THOSE WHO FEAR GOD.

Paul uses similar language when he addresses the congregation at Antioch of Pisidia (Acts 13:16).
It is probable in both cases that the phrase "those who fear God" refers to Jewish proselytes (See
Acts 13:43).

And when we were come to Jerusalem, . . . the Jews which were of Asia, when they saw him in the temple, stirred up all the people, and laid hands on him . . . (For they had seen before with him in the city Trophimus an Ephesian, whom they supposed that Paul had brought into the temple.) . . . and they took Paul, and drew him out of the temple: and forthwith the doors were shut. And as they went about to kill him, tidings came unto the chief captain of the band, that all Jerusalem was in an uproar. . . . and when he could not know the certainty for the tumult, he commanded him to be carried into the castle. And when he came upon the stairs, so it was, that he was borne of the soldiers for the violence of the people. (Acts 21:17, 27, 29, 30, 31, 34, 35)

THE TEMPLE INSCRIPTION

Very few architectural fragments from the Temple of Herod at Jerusalem are known. Of these, two are limestone blocks inscribed in Greek with a warning to foreigners, on pain of death, not to enter the inner courts of the Temple. Josephus states that these warnings, written in both Latin and Greek, were set in a low balustrade at the innermost limit of the first court of the Temple, called the Court of the Gentiles.

One of these blocks, now in the Archaeological Museum at Istanbul, contains the warning complete in seven lines of Greek text. The other—the more recently found inscription, now in the Rockefeller Museum in Jerusalem—is only partly preserved. With the exception of a very slight difference in one word and the fact that the new inscription was inscribed in six lines of Greek rather than seven, the text of both warnings was the same. The broken inscription may be reconstructed to read, when translated:

No foreigner is to enter within the balustrade and enclosure around the Temple area.
Whoever is caught will have himself to blame for his death which will follow.

And when it was day, certain of the Jews banded together, and bound themselves under a curse, saying that they would neither eat nor drink till they had killed Paul. And they were more than forty which had made this conspiracy. . . . So the chief captain . . . called unto him two centurions, saying, Make ready two hundred soldiers to go to Caesarea, . . . And provide them beasts, that they may set Paul on, and bring him safe unto Felix the governor. . . . But after two years Porcius Festus came into Felix' room: and Felix, willing to shew the Jews a pleasure, left Paul bound. . . . Then said Paul, I stand at Caesar's judgment seat, where I ought to be judged: to the Jews have I done no wrong, as thou very well knowest. . . . Then Festus, when he had conferred with the council, answered, Hast thou appealed unto Caesar? unto Caesar shalt thou go. (Acts 23:12–13, 22, 23, 24; 24:27; 25:10, 12)

COIN OF NERO

The Roman emperor to whom Paul made his appeal, and to whom Paul was sent, was Nero (A.D. 54–58), whose full name after his adoption by the Emperor Claudius was Nero Claudius Caesar Drusus Germanicus. Nero was an enthusiastic supporter of art and an avid lover of sports, but his extravagances made him very unpopular. It was rumored that he started the fire that destroyed much of Rome in A.D. 64, and in order to escape the charge of arson, he blamed it on the Christians. In the midst of revolt across the empire in A.D. 68, he fled the throne and committed suicide.

The coin seen here is a tetradrachm issued by the mint in Alexandria and found in Samaria. The obverse has a bust of Nero with radiate crown and his name, NERO, in Greek letters to the left. The reverse of the coin shows the Roman eagle.

And when it was determined that we should sail into Italy, they delivered Paul and certain other prisoners unto one named Julius, a centurion of Augustus' band. And entering into a ship of Adramyttium, we launched, meaning to sail by the coasts of Asia . . . And when we had sailed over the sea of Cilicia and Pamphylia, we came to Myra, a city of Lycia. And there the centurion found a ship of Alexandria sailing into Italy; and he put us therein. And when we had sailed slowly many days, and scarce were come over against Cnidus, the wind not suffering us, we sailed under Crete, over against Salmone; and, hardly passing it, came unto a place which is called The fair havens . . .   (Acts 27:1, 2, 5–7, 8)

VOYAGE TO ROME

Because the prevailing winds along the length of the Mediterranean are westerly, the square-rigged sailing vessels of the first century could sail before the wind eastward with relative ease. The return journey westward was always more difficult. Forced to take advantage of breezes coming off the land, vessels sailing westward stayed near the coast, even at the risk of being blown ashore during a storm.

The constant decision of how to steer the ship along the coast but not too near the shoreline, in order to take advantage of wind and current, was the job of the helmsman. As the decorative medallion from Corinth shows, the helmsman was located in an exposed position high in the stern of the ship where he could control the large steering oar or rudder and determine the ship's heading.

But not long after there arose against it a tempestuous wind, called Euroclydon. And when the ship was caught, and could not bear up into the wind, we let her drive. . . . But when the fourteenth night was come, as we were driven up and down in Adria, about midnight the shipmen deemed that they drew near to some country . . . And falling into a place where two seas met, they ran the ship aground . . . . And when they were escaped, then they knew that the island was called Melita. (Acts 27:14–15, 27, 41; 28:1)

MALTA

By staying in the relatively protected waters found between the mainland and the island of Crete, the vessel on which Paul set sail from Myra on the southern coast of Asia Minor was able to gain the port of Fair Havens on Crete's southern coast. But because the next stage of the voyage was over open water, and because it was already late in the fall of the year (when first-century ships, especially heavily laden grain vessels, did not venture into unsheltered waters), there was hesitancy about continuing before springtime. Having set sail for Rome, however, the vessel was struck by a northeaster. Steps were taken to prevent foundering and breakup of the ship. The vessel was lightened by dumping the cargo of grain overboard and casting secondary tackle and deck equipment adrift. Efforts were made to keep the hull intact by passing ropes under the keel, then up and around the vessel, to both prevent the planks of the hull from springing and to hold the ship's timbers in place. After a fortnight in the storm, it was decided to beach the vessel on a newly observed but unknown shore. The sails were hoisted and the ship was driven onto a peninsula of land, where she was broken up by the surf. All aboard, including passengers and prisoners, made it safely to land.

  The account of Paul's nautical voyage and shipwreck in the Book of Acts is one of the most vivid and detailed in all of ancient literature. St. Paul's Bay, traditional site of the shipwreck, is located on the island of Malta's north shore.

In the same quarters were possessions of the chief man of the island, whose name was Publius; who received us, and lodged us three days courteously. And it came to pass, that the father of Publius lay sick of a fever and of a bloody flux: to whom Paul entered in, and prayed, and laid his hands on him, and healed him. So when this was done, others also, which had diseases in the island, came, and were healed . . . (Acts 28:7-9)

ROMAN VILLA AT MALTA

The museum at Rabat on the island of Malta is built around an elaborate and well-executed floor mosaic of the Roman period. The mosaic's central panel, depicting two birds perched above a golden bowl, is edged with a series of borders. The outermost and widest of these contains a repeated geometric design or maze that gives a striking illusion of depth. A mosaic of this quality would probably have been located in the atrium or one of the more formal rooms of a wealthy citizen's villa.

     While the quarters of Publius, "the chief man of the island" (PRŌTŌS, the first or chief magistrate) have not been identified, it is probable that Paul's host lived in a dwelling comparable to and contemporary with the villa that housed this mosaic.

And after three months we departed in a ship of Alexandria, which had wintered in the isle, whose sign was Castor and Pollux. . . . and so we went toward Rome. (Acts 28:11, 14)

ROME

Rome was concerned with affirming her central place in the first-century world. She demonstrated her power and authority not only with building programs, legions, and laws, but also when and wherever possible through clearly recognizable symbols of strength. As a result, emblems and representations of Roman supremacy are found throughout the Roman world on seals, frescoes, mosaics, the reverse sides of coins, or as part of the decorative motif of buildings. One such depiction is found on a marble block that lies fallen near the first-century-B.C. Theatre of Marcellus. Cut in bas-relief, a Roman eagle standing with spread wings on the orbed end of a scepter is surrounded by the walls, gates, and defense towers of the city of Rome. At a glance, a traveler to the capital would have been reminded that Roman authority, located within the city's defense perimeter, was secure.

And from thence, when the brethren heard of us, they came to meet us as far as Appii forum, and The three taverns: whom when Paul saw, he thanked God, and took courage.
(Acts 28:15)

APPIAN WAY

The repeated passage of chariot and wagon wheels along the Appian Way has caused wide and deep grooves to be worn into its limestone pavers. Begun as early as 312 B.C. by Appius Claudius Caecus, after whom it was named, it is the oldest Roman road known. The Appian Way varies from fourteen to eighteen feet in width and runs from Brundisium on the southeastern coast of Italy to Rome.
Parts of it are still in use.

And when we came to Rome, the centurion delivered the prisoners to the captain of the guard: but Paul was suffered to dwell by himself with a soldier that kept him. (Acts 28:16)

BRIDGES OF THE TIBER

Of the ancient bridges which crossed the Tiber River to Rome, the Pons Fabricius or Ponte Fabricio—
shown here to the right, built by the Roman consul L. Fabricus in 62 B.C.—is one of the oldest.
It remains intact and in use today. Inscriptions on the white marble facings of the arches record the names
and dates of the builder and of persons who have repaired and helped maintain the structure.
The bridge connects Rome's east bank with the Isola Tiberina, an island known in the first century as
Insula Aesculapii because of the presence there of a temple to the god of healing, Aesculapius.
When the Jewish colony settled in the neighboring quarter, the Pons Fabricius was renamed the
Pons Judaeorium.

Construction began on the Pons Aemilius or the Ponte Rotto, shown here to the left, in 181 B.C.
Rome's first stone bridge, it was finished thirty-eight years later. Today just one arch survives.
Both bridges were known to Paul and would have been used often by the early Christian community.

*And it came to pass, that after three days Paul called the chief of the Jews together:
and when they were come together, he said unto them, Men and brethren, though I have
committed nothing against the people, or customs of our fathers, yet was I delivered prisoner
from Jerusalem into the hands of the Romans. . . . for the hope of Israel I am bound with
this chain. . . . And when they had appointed him a day, there came many to him into his
lodging; to whom he expounded and testified the kingdom of God, persuading them
concerning Jesus, both out of the law of Moses, and out of the prophets, from morning
till evening.*   (Acts 28:17, 20, 23)

"HOPE OF ISRAEL"

In A.D. 81, the Roman Senate erected a triumphal arch of Pentalic marble to the Emperor Titus (A.D. 79–81)
to commemorate his capture of Jerusalem in A.D. 70. When a Roman garrison was massacred in
Jerusalem in A.D. 66 during a revolt by the Jews, Rome responded by sending an army under the command
of Vespasian to suppress the uprising. Before the insurgents could be quelled, however, Vespasian
became emperor (A.D. 67–79), and the responsibility of subduing the insurgents was given to his son, Titus.
The thoroughness with which Titus stopped the revolt is reflected in Josephus's account of how
thousands were taken to Rome as slaves. In the course of the fighting, the Temple in Jerusalem caught
fire and was destroyed.

Within the Arch of Titus and on its east facade is a badly damaged bas-relief depicting the
triumphant return of Titus riding in a four-horse chariot crowned by Victory and led by the goddess Roma.
Opposite, on the west facade, a bas-relief depicts a parade of figures carrying booty taken from the
Temple of Jerusalem, including the seven-branched golden menorah and the table of shewbread.
The heavily laden procession appears to move with gathering momentum from left to right, where it passes
under a triumphal arch and out of view.

To Timothy, my dearly beloved son: . . . The cloke that I left at Troas with Carpus, when thou comest, bring with thee, and the books, but especially the parchments. (II Timothy 1:2; 4:13)

Ye see how large a letter I have written unto you with mine own hand. (Galatians 6:11)

The salutation of Paul with mine own hand, which is the token in every epistle: so I write.
(II Thessalonians 3:17)

THE EPISTLES

Paul's letters reached where Paul could not go. Some were written from prison. He once asked his readers to pray for him "that the word of the Lord may have free course" (II Thessalonians 3:1). Most scholars agree that these letters were the beginning of the New Testament as we know it today.

In the first part of this century, in Egypt, the eighty-six-page remains of a papyrus codex or book which contained copies of the letters of Paul were discovered among other materials. Written in the Greek letter style of the third century A.D., these papyrus leaves are among the oldest New Testament manuscript material known. In this codex the letters of Paul are in the unfamiliar order of Romans, Hebrews, I and II Corinthians, Ephesians, Galatians, Philippians, Colossians, and I Thessalonians. The leaves which probably contained II Thessalonians are missing.

The papyrus leaf shown is in the University of Michigan collection (P. Michigan Inv. 6238, P. 46). It contains the last lines of the Letter to the Ephesians and the first line of the Letter to the Galatians, beginning with the familiar words "Paul, an apostle, . . . (not of men, neither by man . . .)."

ΙΝΑ ΑΥΤΟ ΠΑΡΗCΙΑCΩΜΑΙ ΩC ΔΕΙ ΜΕ ΛΑΛΗCΑΙ ΙΝΑ
ΔΕ ΕΙΔΗΤΕ ΤΑ ΚΑΤ ΕΜΕ ΤΙ ΠΡΑCCΩ ΠΑΝΤΑ ΓΝΩ
ΡΙCΕΙ ΥΜΕΙΝ ΤΥΧΙΚΟC Ο ΑΓΑΠΗΤΟC ΑΔΕΛΦΟC ΚΑΙ
ΠΙCΤΟC ΔΙΑΚΟΝΟC ΕΝ ΚΩ ΟΝ ΕΠΕΜΨΑ ΠΡΟC ΥΜΑC
ΕΙC ΑΥΤΟ ΤΟΥΤΟ ΙΝΑ ΓΝΩΤΕ ΤΑ ΠΕΡΙ ΗΜΩΝ ΚΑΙ ΠΑ
ΡΑΚΑΛΕCΗ ΤΑC ΚΑΡΔΙΑC ΗΜΩΝ ΕΙΡΗΝΗ ΤΟΙC ΑΓΙΟC
ΚΑΙ ΑΓΑΠΗ ΜΕΤΑ ΠΙCΤΕΩC ΑΠΟ ΘΥ ΠΡC ΚΑΙ ΚΥ ΙΗΥ
ΧΡΥ Η ΧΑΡΙC ΜΕΤΑ ΠΑΝΤΩΝ ΤΩΝ ΑΓΑΠΩΝΤΩΝ
ΤΟΝ ΚΝ ΗΜΩΝ ΙΗΝ ΧΡΝ ΕΝ ΑΦΘΑΡCΙΑ

ΠΡΟΣ ΓΑΛΑΤΑΣ

ΠΑΥΛΟC ΑΠΟCΤΟΛΟC ΟΥΚ ΑΠ ΑΝΘΡΩΠΩΝ ΟΥΔΕ
ΔΙ ΑΝΘΡΩΠΟΥ ΑΛΛΑ ΔΙΑ ΙΗΥ ΧΡΥ ΚΑΙ ΘΥ ΠΡΟC
ΤΟΥ ΕΓΕΙΡΑΝΤΟC ΑΥΤΟΝ ΕΚ ΝΕΚΡΩΝ ΚΑΙ ΟΙ CΥΝ ΕΜΟΙ
ΠΑΝΤΕC ΑΔΕΛΦΟΙ ΤΑΙC ΕΚΚΛΗCΙΑΙC ΤΗC ΓΑΛΑ
ΤΙΑC ΧΑΡΙC ΥΜΕΙΝ ΚΑΙ ΕΙΡΗΝΗ ΑΠΟ ΘΥ ΠΡC
ΚΑΙ ΚΥ ΗΜΩΝ ΙΗΥ ΧΡΥ ΤΟΥ ΔΟΝΤΟC ΑΥΤΟΝ ΠΕΡΙ
ΑΜΑΡΤΙΩΝ ΗΜΩΝ ΟΠΩC ΕΞΕΛΗΤΑΙ ΗΜΑC ΕΚ
ΑΙΩΝΟC ΤΟΥ ΕΝΕCΤΩΤΟC ΠΟΝΗΡΟΥ ΚΑΤΑ ΤΟ ΘΕ
ΛΗΜΑ ΤΟΥ ΘΥ ΚΑΙ ΠΡC ΗΜΩΝ Ω Η ΔΟΞΑ ΕΙC ΤΟΥC
ΑΙΩΝΩΝ ΑΜΗΝ ΘΑΥΜΑΖΩ ΟΤΙ ΟΥΤΩC
ΤΑΧΕΩC ΜΕΤΑΤΙΘΕCΘΕ ΑΠΟ ΤΟΥ ΚΑΛΕCΑΝΤΟC ΥΜΑC
ΕΙC ΕΤΕΡΟΝ ΕΥΑΓΓΕΛΙΟΝ Ο ΟΥΚ ΕCΤΙΝ ΑΛ
ΛΟ ΕΙ ΜΗ ΤΙΝΕC ΕΙCΙΝ ΟΙ ΤΑΡΑCCΟΝΤΕC ΥΜΑC ΚΑΙ
ΘΕΛΟΝΤΕC ΜΕΤΑCΤΡΕΨΑΙ ΤΟ ΕΥΑΓΓΕΛΙΟΝ ΤΟΥ ΧΡΥ

At my first answer no man stood with me, but all men forsook me: . . . Notwithstanding the Lord stood with me, and strengthened me; . . . and I was delivered out of the mouth of the lion. (II Timothy 4:16, 17)

For I am now ready to be offered, and the time of my departure is at hand. I have fought a good fight, I have finished my course, I have kept the faith . . . (II Timothy 4:6, 7)

OSTIAN WAY

In the late first century B.C., a 117-foot-high marble-covered pyramid was built beside the Via Ostiensis, a 14-mile-long road leading from the capital to Ostia, the port of Rome. Reflecting Rome's growing interest in her new province of Egypt, the pyramid was erected as a funerary monument to the praetor (judge) Cestius.

The crenellated top of the late city-gate tower, seen here to the lower right, marks the location of the Porta Ostiensis, Rome's Ostian Gate.

Eusebius in his *Ecclesiastical History* (II. xxv) written about A.D. 311 records this tradition: "It is related that in his (Nero's) time Paul was beheaded in Rome itself." He then quotes an earlier writing as associating this with "the Ostian Way."

If the tradition is accurate, Paul would have left Rome by the Ostian Gate and passed by the pyramid of Cestius on the way to execution.

I John, who also am your brother, and companion in tribulation, and in the kingdom and patience of Jesus Christ, was . . . in the Spirit on the Lord's day, and heard behind me a great voice, as of a trumpet, saying . . . (Revelation 1:9, 10, 11)

THE APOCALYPSE

Unto the angel of the church of Ephesus write . . . do the first works; or else I will come unto thee quickly, and will remove thy candlestick out of his place, except thou repent. . . . To him that overcometh will I give to eat of the tree of life, which is in the midst of the paradise of God. (Revelation 2:1, 5, 7)

CANDLESTICK AT EPHESUS

In marked contrast to the extensive ruins of ancient Ephesus, little evidence remains of Christian or Jewish communities from the first and second centuries A.D. One small bit of such evidence, however, has been found at the Library of Celsus, an early second-century building now undergoing restoration. Scratched into the surface of one of its nine thirty-five-foot-wide marble steps, is a seven-branched candlestick or menorah.

And unto the angel of the church in Smyrna write . . . be thou faithful unto death, and I will give thee a crown of life. . . . He that overcometh shall not be hurt of the second death.
(Revelation 2:8, 10, 11)

LIONS OF SMYRNA

The two lions, which appear to stalk through the grass of a field, are on the site of the forum of the ancient Roman capital city of Smyrna. Originally part of the decorative motif of an unidentified building, they serve as grim reminders of the fate of certain Christians in the first three centuries. As punishment for subversion, antisocial behavior, or simply for their belief, Christians were fed to wild beasts or compelled to fight lions in the public arena. Such was the fate of Polycarp, bishop of Smyrna, whom Eusebius calls "the companion of the Apostles." The crowd attending the games in the stadium at Smyrna demanded that Polycarp (circa A.D. 96–155), then eighty-six years of age, be thrown to the lions. The Asiarch—Philip of Tralles—refused, saying that the games at Smyrna were officially over. When the crowd then demanded that Polycarp be burned, the Proconsul Statius Quodratus agreed, unless the elderly man recanted. Polycarp responded, "Change of mind from better to worse is a change we may not make." And he was martyred in the city where he had served as bishop for forty years.

And to the angel of the church in Pergamos write . . . thou dwellest, even where Satan's seat is: and thou holdest fast my name . . . But I have a few things against thee . . . Repent . . . To him that overcometh will I give to eat of the hidden manna, and will give him a white stone, and in the stone a new name written, which no man knoweth saving he that receiveth it. (Revelation 2:12, 13, 14, 16, 17)

PERGAMUM

The Temple of Aesculapius, god of healing, and its associated therapeutic center, comprising in part a theatre, library, bath and gymnasium, mark the site where the finest medicine was practiced in the first century A.D. The shattered remains of these structures lie a short distance southwest of the one-quarter mile high granite massif atop which the city of Pergamum was built. From the hospital complex, the steep Greek-style theatre of Pergamum with its seventy-eight rows of rock-carved seats can be seen beside the city, high on the southwest face of the mountain.

In the first century one of the great libraries of the ancient world stood directly behind the theatre. It contained as many as 200,000 volumes until Mark Antony gave the collection to Cleopatra and the books were removed to the Museum at Alexandria where at a later date they were all destroyed by fire. Located to the right of the theatre was the glistening white 120-foot-wide altar of Zeus, clearly visible in the first century both from the Aesculapium and from miles beyond. Adorned with an elaborate white marble frieze (now in the Berlin Museum), the altar depicted the massive struggle between the gods and the giants and symbolized for the world the defense of civilization made by the kings of Pergamum against the barbarians, particularly the Gauls.

It has been suggested that "Satan's seat" referred to in the Book of Revelation is a reference to the altar of Zeus at Pergamum. At the same time, the obvious parallel between the symbol of Aesculapius, a serpent, found throughout the city and John's synonym for Satan, "that old serpent" (Revelation 12:9), would hardly have been lost on the Christian residents of Pergamum.

*And unto the angel of the church in Thyatira write . . . I am he which searcheth the reins
and hearts: and I will give unto every one of you according to your works. . . .
And he that overcometh, and keepeth my works unto the end, to him will I give power over
the nations: And he shall rule them with a rod of iron . . . And I will give him the morning star.*
(Revelation 2:18, 23, 26, 27, 28)

THYATIRA

In the Turkish town of Akhisar, digging associated with road repairs led to the discovery of a long line of
fallen columns and arches such as are shown here. These architectural fragments are thought to be part
of the colonnade that paralleled the main north-south street (*cardo maximus*) of the city of Thyatira.
Since the majority of these remains date from the Roman period, and all apparently fell at about the same
time, it has been assumed that Thyatira suffered such a devastating earthquake that the city along
the *cardo maximus* was not rebuilt.

And unto the angel of the church in Sardis write . . . Be watchful . . . for I have not found thy works perfect before God . . . Thou hast a few names even in Sardis which have not defiled their garments . . . for they are worthy. He that overcometh, the same shall be clothed in white raiment; and I will not blot out his name out of the book of life . . . (Revelation 3:1, 2, 4, 5)

SARDIS

One of the oldest cities of Asia Minor, and long the capital of the kingdom of Lydia, Sardis was founded beside the 5,900-foot-high Mount Tmolos. Its location enabled the city to build a triple-walled acropolis deemed to be unassailable on top of a steep, 800-foot-high northern spur of the mountain. By observing that birds could roost undisturbed on certain sections of the acropolis walls, however, and concluding that those sections were unmanned and unwatched, the Persians were able to scale the walls and capture the acropolis. Thus, Croesus, King of Lydia, and all his wealth came under the control of Cyrus, King of the Persians. Sardis capitulated to Alexander the Great in 334 B.C. and was granted independence, a condition that lasted a brief twelve years and was not regained until over a century later. Finally, Attalus III (139–133 B.C.), King of Pergamum, willed his kingdom—including Sardis—to Rome. Under the Romans, the city continued to grow in splendor and importance until A.D. 17, when it was destroyed by a major earthquake. In the time of the Apostles, Sardis was rebuilding, but would never regain its ancient glory.

To the west and below the acropolis lie the remains of the massive 326-foot-long by 163-foot-wide Temple of Artemis (Cybele), the building of which dates back to 300 B.C. Of the original 64 Ionic columns, two are intact and standing. Crosses carved into the temple's facade indicate that it was once used as a Christian Church.

And to the angel of the church in Philadelphia write . . . behold, I have set before thee an open door, and no man can shut it: for thou hast a little strength, and hast kept my word, and hast not denied my name. . . hold that fast which thou hast, that no man take thy crown. Him that overcometh will I make a pillar in the temple of my God . . . and I will write upon him the name of my God, and the name of the city of my God, which is new Jerusalem, which cometh down out of heaven from my God: and I will write upon him my new name. (Revelation 3:7, 8, 11, 12)

WALLS OF PHILADELPHIA

Founded by Attalos II of Pergamum (150–138 B.C.), Philadelphia was located on a plateau overlooking the Cogamus Valley, along which ran the imperial post road between Sardis and Laodicea. The remains of the city are now almost entirely covered by the modern town of Alaşehir. Outlines of a Roman theatre, a gymnasium, and a stadium can still be traced amid the shops and homes of the present inhabitants. The most evident of the archaeological remains of Philadelphia are sections of the city wall which originally surrounded it.

And unto the angel of the church of the Laodiceans write . . . thou art neither cold nor hot . . .
So then because thou art lukewarm, and neither cold nor hot, I will spue thee out of my
mouth. . . . Behold, I stand at the door, and knock . . . To him that overcometh will I grant
to sit with me in my throne, even as I also overcame, and am set down with my Father
in his throne. . . .
HE THAT HATH AN EAR, LET HIM HEAR WHAT THE SPIRIT SAITH UNTO THE CHURCHES.
(Revelation 3:14, 15, 16, 20, 21–22)

WARM WATER AT LAODICEA

The ruined remains of a water tower and bath lie in the center of the mound at Laodicea. Originally these constructions were connected by a large aqueduct and siphon made up of fitted limestone blocks pierced through the center with ceramic pipe. This system brought warm water to the city from the spring, Baspinar, located four miles to the south. At regular intervals in the siphon, funnel-shaped holes cut from the upper surface of the stone block tapped the central pipe. These openings were designed to serve not only as a means of determining the location of blockage in the pipe but also, when fitted with rounded stones, as a means of insuring continued water pressure within the siphon. Laden with calcium and sodium carbonates, and sodium chlorides, the warm spring water frequently caused the interior of the pipes to become clogged with deposits. Evidence of such residue can be seen in the broken pipes shown here.

CONVERSE COUNTY LIBRARY
DOUGLAS, WYOMING

And the Spirit
and the bride say, Come.
And let him
that heareth say, Come.
And let him
that is athirst come.
And whosoever will,
let him take the
water of life freely.
(Revelation 22:17)